EXPLORE

The World of
SNAKES

Chris Mattison

DERRYDALE BOOKS
New York

A SALAMANDER BOOK

First published by Salamander Books Ltd.,
129-137 York Way, London N7 9LG,
United Kingdom.

© Salamander Books Ltd. 1991

ISBN 0-517-05912-6

8 7 6 5 4 3 2 1

This 1991 edition published by Derrydale Books, distributed by
Outlet Book Company, Inc., 225 Park Avenue South,
New York, New York 10003.

Printed and bound in Belgium.

CREDITS

Edited by: The Book Creation Company Ltd.

Designed by: Philip Mann

Artwork by: Dennis Ovenden

Color separation by: P & W Graphics, Pte. Ltd., Singapore

Printed by: Proost International Book Production, Turnhout,
Belgium

CONTENTS

THE WORLD OF SNAKES

People are probably more frightened of snakes than any other type of animal. They have a reputation of being slimy, poisonous and ready to attack at the earliest possible moment.

Recently, however, we have come to realize that snakes are just as interesting as other animals and should be treated with respect.

The First Snakes

The oldest fossils of snakes show that a type of snake existed between 100 and 150 million years ago.

The remains of the longest snake that ever lived date back about 36 million years, and were found in Egypt. By studying them scientists believe that this snake was about 60 feet (18 metres) long.

What Is A Snake?

Today there are about 2,500 types of snake, but new ones are being found all the time. They belong to a group called reptiles, who all breathe air, have scales, and either give birth to live young or lay eggs.

▼ Snakes are thought to have evolved from burrowing lizards.

▶ The legless lizard cannot be mistaken for a snake because it has eyelids and several rows of scales along its belly.

Like us, snakes are vertebrates. That means that they have a backbone and a nervous system that runs from the brain down the spine.

Snake Or Legless Lizard?
Land snakes have a single row of wide scales running right down their bellies. These are known as the

◀ The spur-like claws that can be seen on either side of boas and pythons are the remains of legs.

ventral scales and they help snakes to move. Lizards have various arrangements of scales on their bellies, but never a single row. Snakes do not have eyelids – their eyes are covered with a single transparent scale, but lizards, on the other hand, do have movable eyelids. Finally, snakes do not have eardrums, whereas most lizards do.

▲ Snakes have no movable eyelids, no eardrums and their bellies are covered with broad ventral scales.

LIFE WITHOUT LEGS

Although there aren't any snakes with legs, and all are generally long and thin, it is possible to tell most of the 2,500 species apart by looking at their different sizes, shapes, colours and markings.

Smallest And Largest
The smallest snakes are the ones that live underground. They are called burrowing snakes. Several of these snakes are less than 10 inches (25 cm) long, and some are even less than 6 inches (15 cm) long. All are as thin as bootlaces. Burrowing snakes spend their lives beneath the surface hunting for ants, termites and other insects on which to feed.

▲ All the largest snakes belong to the python or boa families. The Burmese python may grow to more than 20 feet (6 metres).

The largest snakes belong to the boa and python families. These snakes are not poisonous. The longest python from South-East Asia can grow up to 30 feet (9 metres) long. In South America, the anaconda grows almost as long, but is much fatter.

Other large snakes include the African python and the Indian or Burmese python, which grows to 21 feet (6.5 metres). The common boa, or boa constrictor, is often thought to be the biggest snake in the world. But in fact these snakes never grow

Snakes range from less than 6 ins (15cm) to almost 30 feet (9 metres) in length.

longer than about 20 feet (6 metres). They are only fifth or sixth in the world league table of giant snakes!

Fat Or Thin

The shapes of snakes vary from long and slender, to squat with a blunt head and a short tail. Some snakes have broad, spade-shaped heads,

▲ **The long nosed tree snake is well adapted to life among the branches of trees and bushes.**

while others, such as tree snakes, have a long snout which ends in a sharp point.

There are extremes, but most snakes are between 18 ins and 7 feet long (0.5 and 2 metres), moderately slender and with a long tapering tail.

Scales

All snakes are covered in scales. Many people think that snakes are slimy, but in fact they are dry and warm to the touch. Scales are made up of a substance called keratin, which is what your fingernails are made from. Every scale on a snake's body grows from a thickened area of the outer layer of skin. This

is different from fish scales, which grow on top of the skin and can be removed quite easily. A snake's head, body and tail have different shaped scales.

Most snakes have large, round plate-like scales on their heads, while along the back and sides the scales are shaped like shields and arranged rather like the tiles on a roof. Along the belly are the ventral scales. These are arranged in a single row and help the snake to move.

POISONOUS SNAKES

The largest venomous, or poisonous, snake is the king cobra. It can grow up to 16 feet (4.8 metres). Other long venomous snakes include the black mamba, which is only slightly smaller than the king cobra, and the bushmaster from Central and South America. This snake grows up to 10 feet (3 metres) long.

LIFE WITHOUT LEGS

Moving Without Legs

Most snakes move about on land and in water by wriggling their bodies from side to side. This is called the 'serpentine' movement. The scales on the sides and underside of the snake's body 'grip' onto bumps on the ground or push against the water, pulling the snake along.

▶ **The North American sidewinder is a rattlesnake with an unusual method of moving across sand.**

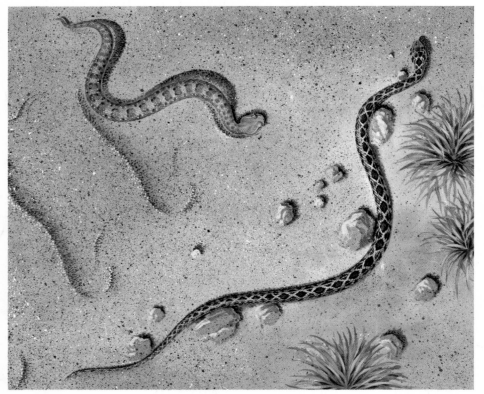

◀ **This drawing shows a sidewinding movement, and the more common 'serpentine' movement used on rough ground.**

When travelling more slowly many larger species of snake crawl in a straight line. They do this by hooking the ventral scales onto rough ground thereby pulling the body forward. This gives the effect of a series of waves moving along the snake's belly.

Specialist Movement

Snakes that live in deserts or other sandy parts of the world cannot grip onto the unstable sand surface, so they have to throw their bodies across the sand in a series of loops. The head lifts off the ground, followed by the body and finally the tail.

This movement is called sidewinding, and the snakes that move in this way are known as sidewinders.

Colour

One of the best ways of telling one species of snake from another is through their colours and markings. These are made by special cells in each scale, and can produce some breathtaking patterns.

▼ **The sunbeam snake, from South East Asia, has highly polished and beautiful scales.**

THE CALIFORNIAN KINGSNAKE

The Californian kingsnake is a good example of a snake whose colour is thought to act as a defence against predators. This snake is common in western North America. In most of the areas it lives the kingsnake's black and white colouring is arranged into bands or rings around the body and tail. But in one area the markings of half the kingsnakes are arranged in a thick white stripe along the back and two more along each side. At first scientists thought the snakes were not the same species, but then it was shown that both types could hatch from the same clutch of eggs. Striped parents could produce banded offspring.

Scientists believe that if a predator, such as a hawk, has eaten a striped kingsnake, in future the hawk will look for the striped type and overlook the banded or ringed ones.

Sometimes the colour blends in with the surroundings of the snake making it hard for predators to spot. Alternatively, the colour may warn predators that a particular snake is poisonous.

The Senses

The way a snake sees, hears and smells is quite different to other animals. Although most have poor eyesight, some snakes can focus both eyes on one spot enabling them to strike accurately at their prey.

LIFE WITHOUT LEGS

Hearing Without Ears
Snakes do not have ears, and are therefore deaf. But a snake's body is always in contact with the ground or the branch of a tree, so they are very sensitive to vibrations. These are sensed in the lower jaw and carried to the brain through a single earbone.

Smelling
Snakes flick their tongues when they are disturbed or hunting, because it is collecting tiny scent particles. These are transferred to a pair of small pits in the roof of the mouth. They form part of a small structure called the Jacobson's organ. This is connected directly to the brain and provides an excellent sense of smell.

Heat Detection
Rattlesnakes, and most boas and pythons, have a series of heat-sensitive pits running along both sides of their heads which can detect a warm object. By comparing the 'messages' received on either side of its head, these snakes can work out the exact

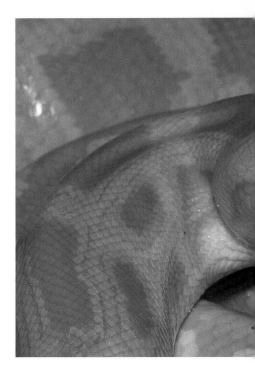

▼ This young emerald boa has many heat-sensitive pits, helping it to hunt in the dark.

▲ This ratsnake is flicking its tongue to pick up scent, which will be passed to its Jacobson's organ.

position of an object, striking accurately in total darkness.

Skeleton

The skull of a snake is long and narrow, and is made up of many delicate bones. Some are only loosely attached to each other, so the mouth can be opened much wider.

The bones of the spine are called vertebrae. They are all similar in shape and size, and are linked to each other by ball and socket joints.

◀ **Most pythons have rows of heat-sensitive organs along their head to detect small rises in temperature.**

Muscles connect the ribs to the spine, skin and scales. Others link the scales on the side of a snake's body to the ventral scales. By contracting all these muscles in turn, the snake is able to move along.

FACT FILE

● The snake's backbone is very flexible and strong.
● The number of vertebrae varies from 165 to 435 depending on the snake.
● Humans have 32 vertebrae!

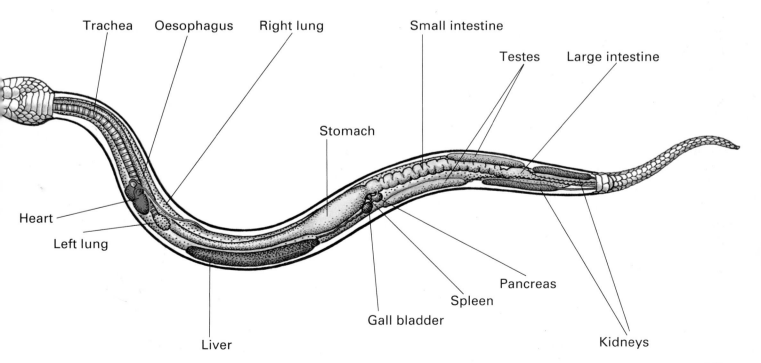

Trachea Oesophagus Right lung Small intestine Testes Large intestine

Stomach

Heart

Left lung

Pancreas

Spleen

Gall bladder

Kidneys

Liver

FOOD AND FEEDING

The giant constricting snakes, such as boas and pythons, can eat small deer, cats, dogs and, very occasionally, humans. The anaconda of South America spends some of its time in water and will eat turtles and even alligators!

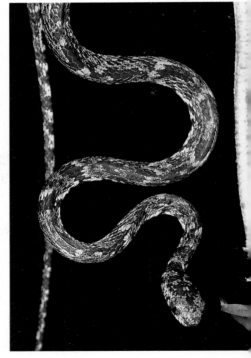

All snakes are predators. They hunt, kill and eat other animals. Most species of snakes prefer to feed on just two or three types of animals. The European grass snake feeds mainly on fish or frogs, whereas the North American corn snake eats small rodents such as mice.

There are, however, a few species that are less fussy about what they eat, so

▲ The long-nosed tree-snake feeds mainly on lizards, which it hunts among the branches where it lives.

long as the animal is small enough to kill and swallow. The North American kingsnake will eat lizards, rodents, birds, frogs and even other snakes. Larger snakes, because of their strength, can hunt a greater variety of prey.

▲ The snail-eating snake is long and slender. This enables it to climb in search of tree-snails.

Specialized Feeders

There are a few species of snakes that will only eat one type of food. The cat-eyed snake from Central and South America will eat lizards and frogs, but its favourite meal is frogs' eggs. In this part of the world there are types of frogs that lay their eggs on leaves which overhang water, making them an easy meal.

Snail Eaters

In North, Central and South America, Africa and South-East Asia, there are groups of snakes that feed only on snails. Because of the hard shells, snakes have to find ways of getting to the soft, fleshy bits inside. Some species have special skulls that allow the snake to thrust its lower jaw inside the shell and then pull it back, bringing out the animal inside. Other types wedge the shell under a rock and then twist their bodies until the snail is pulled out. A third group of snakes grasps the fleshy part and then bashes it against a rock until the shell breaks.

The African Egg-eating Snake

The most specialized feeder of all the snakes is the African egg-eating snake. This snake will eat nothing but eggs. They have very elastic jaws which can swallow a bird's egg much larger than their heads. There are also special vertebrae which have tiny spikes jutting out into the throat. By moving its neck from side to side, the snake can saw through the egg-shell. As soon as the shell breaks, the yolk runs down into the snake's stomach and the shell is pushed back out.

▼ The African egg-eating snake can eat eggs which are larger than its head.

FOOD AND FEEDING

◄ Pit vipers have heat-sensitive organs on each side of their heads between the eyes and the nostrils.

Killing A Catch

Once a snake has caught an animal the next problem it faces is killing it, or keeping it still long enough for it to be swallowed. The first line of attack is a snake's teeth. All

---

FACT FILE

Unlike humans, a snake's teeth are replaced continually throughout its life. This ensures that a snake always has strong, sharp teeth that don't have a chance to wear down.

Finding Prey

Snakes use a combination of sight, sound and smell to find their prey. Those which have them also use heat-sensitive pits. Snakes will either sit and wait for a suitable animal to come within reach, or else they will hunt and chase.

Day And Night Hunters

Snakes that hunt and chase their prey can be divided into two types. Those that hunt during the day, and others that hunt at night.

Daytime hunters tend to have better eyesight and are fast moving. They crawl around in likely places hoping to flush small lizards or other animals out into the open.

Snakes that hunt at night will usually prowl around poking their heads into cracks and crevices where they may well find sleeping lizards or mice.

snakes have sharp, pointed teeth, which often curve backwards so that the snake can get a better grip on its prey.

Most snakes have very fast reactions and can strike out very quickly. Once its prey is within reach it stands little chance of escape. If the prey is a small defenceless animal, such as a grasshopper or frog, the snake can swallow its victim at once.

▶ The sptting cobra can spray venom from the front of its fangs, but hunts by biting as normal.

However, if the prey poses a threat to the snake, or is too big to swallow alive, then the snake has to find a way of killing it or at the very least making it unable to fight back.

CONSTRICTION

These snakes have long, very strong bodies which they use to coil around their victim. They don't crush their victims to death, but simply tighten the coils gradually every time the animal breathes out. In the end the animal cannot breathe and so dies of suffocation. The coils are then relaxed and the snake searches for the animal's head and begins to swallow.

Venom

The saliva of all snakes contains chemicals called enzymes and proteins. These chemicals help snakes to digest the food they eat. In some species the saliva is very powerful and is called venom. It is the venom of a snake's bite that can act like a poison as soon as it enters the victim's blood.

Some venom acts on the blood of a victim, stopping it from clotting or causing it to form massive clots, which may in turn affect the heart. Other types of venom act on the nervous system, and may cause the heart to stop beating or the victim to stop breathing. Generally, a viper's venom acts on the blood, and a cobra's on the nervous system, but there are exceptions.

17

◄ The mangrove snake has fangs in the back of its mouth and needs to chew its prey in order to kill it.

Injecting Venom

Snakes that produce deadly venom need a way of making sure that the venom gets into the victim's bloodstream. Such snakes have special teeth called fangs.

Fortunately, the largest group of venomous snakes have a fairly inefficient way of delivering venom into the bloodstream. Their fangs grow towards the back of the mouth, and these snakes are known as 'back-fanged' snakes. Fangs are usually slightly larger than the rest of the teeth and most have a groove along which the venom flows. Because the fangs, and therefore the venom, are at the back of the mouth, back-fanged snakes have to grip the victim and chew slightly before the venom can enter the bloodstream through the wound. This means that very few back-fanged snakes are dangerous to people.

Natural Needles

Snakes such as cobras, mambas, coral and sea snakes have a more efficient way of injecting venom. All of these species have two fixed fangs growing right at the front of the mouth. Each fang is hollow and the venom is forced through the fang and out through a tiny hole near the tip. It works just like a needle used for injecting people in hospital. This ensures that with just one bite these snakes can inject enough venom to kill or paralyze their victims.

Viper Fangs

The most advanced fangs belong to the group of snakes called vipers. Their fangs are hollow and very long. The

A VIPER'S FANGS

The hinge is a series of free moving bones acting as levers. The fangs are fixed into one rotating bone, which gets pushed forward by a long bone in the top jaw erecting the fangs.

viper has a hinged arrangement in its mouth that allows it to fold its fangs up against the roof of its mouth when they are not being used.

Swallowing

Snakes cannot chew their food so they have to swallow it whole. Most snakes can swallow animals larger than the size of their mouths.

As a snake begins to swallow large prey the jaws dislocate and move separately. First one side and then the other is swung forward to grip the prey, pulling it into the throat. Large prey are usually swallowed head first so that the legs fold back making the prey easier to swallow.

The time taken to swallow a meal varies with its size. A medium-sized ratsnake will take about five minutes to swallow a mouse, whereas a python swallowing a small deer may take over an hour.

▼ Vipers, such as this African bush viper, have long fangs which can be folded out of the way.

SNAKES AS PREY

Although we usually think of snakes as the hunters, there are animals that hunt snakes.

Predators include foxes, mongooses, hedgehogs, meerkats, birds such as owls, hawks, eagles, and even other types of snakes themselves.

Snakes greatest enemies, however, are people. This is mostly out of fear, but in some parts of the world humans hunt snakes for food.

Snakes have many ways of protecting themselves. Most species are coloured to blend in with their natural habitat. So when a snake senses danger it just stays very still.

▼ Most snakes are camouflaged according to the type of place where they live.

20

Markings

Many snakes have markings on their heads and tails, which help disguise them even more. These are usually dark or light bars (especially across the eyes) and patches of colour on the head and body. When resting they are almost impossible to see.

Some snakes change at every stage of their lives. They could start life with blotches and end up with stripes. Others change colour and some do both. But once a snake has changed it cannot change back.

Camouflage

There are several different types of snake camouflage. Most species match their surroundings. They may be green to match the leaves, or brown to match the bark of the trees or the soil and fallen leaves.

Deserts vary in colour, so snakes of the same species can be yellow, brown or red, depending on the sand or gravel type.

Snakes can change the outline of their bodies. They can be coiled up, stretched out, or anything in between. This means that animals hunting snakes never know what they are looking for.

▲ The gaboon viper has a broken pattern which helps it to blend in with dead leaves on the forest floor.

▼ Sidewinders' markings and colours always match the colour of the sand or gravel where they live.

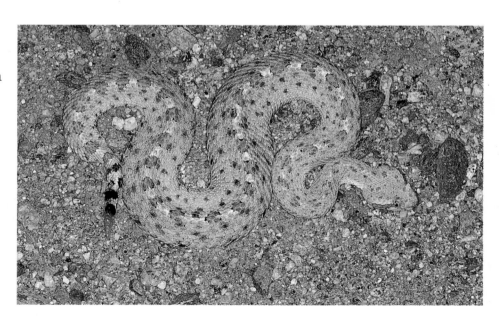

SNAKES AS PREY

Warning Colours

Another way in which a snake's colour can act as a defence is the opposite of camouflage. It involves using bright colours as a warning to predators. Some animals are brightly coloured because they are poisonous or taste nasty if eaten. But snakes do not use colours in quite the same way. Venomous snakes are brightly coloured to warn enemies that they can give a poisonous bite.

The most famous species to use this tactic are coral snakes from North, Central and South America. There are others with warning colours in Africa, Asia and Australia.

▶ **When threatened, the American ringneck snake raises its tail to show its bright underside.**

MIMICS

Kingsnakes and milksnakes are often said to be mimics of the venomous coral snakes. Mimics look like venomous snakes so predators will avoid them. Scientists believe that both types of snake are making use of animals' instinctive knowledge that all brightly coloured animals, such as wasps, bees and some caterpillars, should be avoided. If this is true then all brightly coloured animals could be said to be mimicking each other.

Another theory is that these snakes are all very secretive and live beneath rocks or logs, or in burrows. If an animal discovered one of these snakes by accident, the brilliant colours would flash past the animal's eyes as the snake escaped. This would startle the animal and so give the snake a few extra seconds to escape.

▲ **Red, yellow and orange are often used as warning colours in the animal kingdom.**

Hiding And Warning
Some species of snake use warning colours only as a second line of defence. Such snakes use camouflage, but if this fails they switch to warning colours. The ringneck snakes of North America are brown, grey or black on top but bright red underneath. If discovered they twist their tails into a corkscrew shape exposing the red. A cobra is not brightly coloured, but if threatened it opens its hood to reveal very distinctive warning markings.

The most common colours are black, red, orange, white and yellow. Some species have two colours, while others have three. The colours are always arranged to contrast with each other so they can be seen from a distance. Predators instinctively avoid these species, just as we avoid wasps.

Mimics
Some harmless snakes are also coloured in the same way as poisonous snakes. Predators then think that these snakes are also poisonous and so avoid them. Snakes such as these are known as mimics.

◄ **The cobra raises its body and spreads its hood in order to frighten its enemies.**

23

SNAKES AS PREY

Warning Sounds

Nearly all snakes make a hissing sound if they are threatened. Species such as the North American bull snake have a flap of skin in the wind pipe which makes their hiss even louder and more frightening. Certain small vipers from Africa, the saw-scaled and the horned viper, make a rasping noise by rubbing their coils together. The scales are very rough, and the noise they make sounds like two pieces of sandpaper rubbing together.

But by far the most famous warning sound is made by the rattlesnakes of North, Central and South America. The rattle is thought to have stopped the snakes from being trampled on by the large animals, such as bison, which used to roam over the areas where the rattlesnakes lived.

THE RATTLESNAKE'S RATTLE

The rattlesnake's tail scale is shaped like an egg-timer and the narrow part in the middle holds the scale onto the tail when the skin is shed. Before this happens again the tail shrinks slightly, but the scale stays the same size. It is only loosely held in place and can move. A new scale then forms over the tail, inside the first scale. This process is repeated until the rattle is formed.

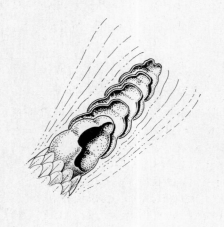

Playing Dead

There are some species of snake that pretend to be dead if they think that they are about to be attacked. This is another form of protection. The European grass snake and the North American hognose snake are the most famous of these types of snake. They roll over onto their backs, open their mouths and let their tongues dangle out. Their instinct to play dead is so strong that if they are turned the right way up, they will roll straight back over again! In addition, the grass snake lets off a foul-smelling substance which makes it smell as if it is dead and rotting. When the danger has passed the snake gradually rolls over and crawls away.

▼ As a warning, the saw-scaled viper produces a loud rasping noise by moving its coils in opposite directions.

Counter-Attack And Bluff

If camouflage, warning colours, warning sounds and other forms of defence do not work, and the snake cannot reach safety, a snake will often put up a show of aggression. Even the smallest snakes huff and puff, open their mouths and make repeated strikes with their head. This aggressive play-acting is intended to frighten the attacker away. If the snake is harmless this aggressive behaviour is a sort of bluff. The snake pretends that it is more dangerous than it really is.

Another type of bluff involves making the attacker strike at the wrong end of the snake. Some burrowing snakes, for example, use their blunt tails as decoys. These snakes raise their tails in the air and wave them around to make them look like heads. Sometimes they will even make striking movements

▲ The Indian sand boa has a blunt tail which is used as a 'false head' so enemies attack the wrong end!

with their tails. In this way, while the attacker is concentrating on the tail, the snake has its head hidden in its coils, where it can start burrowing into the ground for safety. Many of these snakes often have scars on their tails, where they have been bitten by an attacker.

SNAKE REPRODUCTION

Animals reproduce so that their family will survive. The reproductive cycle begins when animals are sexually mature. The cycle consists of finding a mate, courtship, mating and finally egg-laying or birth. The cycle is completed only when the offspring are sexually mature themselves and can, in turn, reproduce.

Courtship
Courtship is when one animal, usually the male, attracts a female with which he can mate. In some species of snake the males have fights or 'combat dances' during the breeding season. The rival males twist and rear up

▼ Some snakes, such as garter snakes, have live young. Others lay eggs.

together, each trying to force the other to the ground. The eventual winner remains and mates with the female.

Mating

If the female is ready to mate she lets off a strong-smelling scent. With this 'perfume' she lays down a trail. The male follows this scent trail until he catches up with the female, and then attempts to mate.

In snakes, mating consists of the male crawling along the back of the female, while trying to persuade her to lift her tail. If the female wants to mate, she lifts her tail, allowing the male to twist his tail beneath hers.

Birth And Egg-laying

The sperm that the male introduces into the female may fertilize the eggs which are already forming inside her, or it may be stored for up to several months. Fertilization means that the group of cells inside the egg, called an embryo, start to develop and grow into a tiny snake.

Depending on the type of snake, one of two things may happen. In some species a shell forms around the egg while it is still in the female's body. These eggs are then laid between one to two months

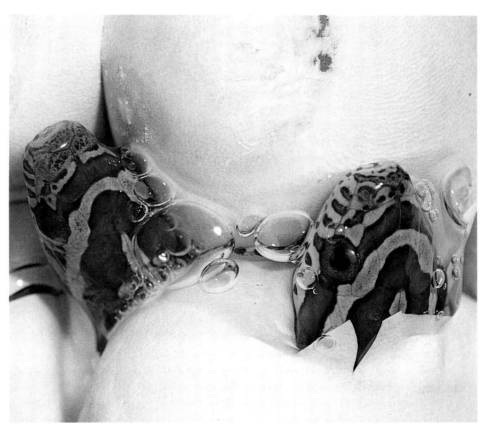

later. The baby snake continues to grow until it hatches. The shells of snakes' eggs are not hard and brittle, like those of a bird, but soft and leathery.

In other species, however, the eggs are kept inside the body of the female until the baby snakes are fully formed, at which point they are born alive. The eggs of these species do not have a shell around them, but only a thin layer of cells called a

▲ These two young cornsnakes are hatching about two months after the eggs have been laid.

membrane. The membrane breaks during the birth or soon afterwards.

Snakes that give birth to living young are called 'viviparous' and include rattlesnakes, vipers and boas. Egg-laying snakes are known as 'oviparous' and include pythons and kingsnakes.

SNAKE REPRODUCTION

sunshine on warm days, or by burrowing underground on cold days and during the night. By keeping them warm in this way, the snakes can develop safely and quickly.

Growth And Development

Unlike mammals, such as humans, snakes do not stop growing once they reach sexual maturity. They grow throughout their lives. Snakes start to breed when they are

◄ This green tree python has remained with her clutch, which is just starting to hatch.

Eggs Or Live Young?

Snakes in eggs will only grow if the temperature outside the egg is about 30°C. If the female is a species that lives somewhere warm, then she can lay her eggs in a sheltered place and let the sun keep them warm until they hatch. But if the female lives in a cooler region she has to keep the 'eggs' inside her body, and find the warmest place for as long as possible. She can do this by laying out in the

► A Baird's ratsnake, from Texas, in the process of laying her eggs in a dark, secluded place.

about half the length that they may eventually become, and are about two or three years old. Larger species of snakes may take longer, while the smaller species, particularly those that live in tropical places, may be sexually mature after a year or less.

Snakes' scales cannot stretch, so they have to shed their skins several times a year as they grow longer. Newly born or hatched snakes shed the outer layer of skin when they are a few days old,

FACT FILE

● Medium-sized snakes, such as kingsnakes live between 10 and 20 years.
● Larger types of snake, such as boas and pythons, may live as long as 30 years.

CHANGING SKIN

Snakes shed their skins because their scales are not flexible. Shedding its skin is made easier by an oily substance that appears between the old and new skins. The snake starts shedding its skin by rubbing its head on a rough object, such as a stone, until the top layer of scales is broken. The snake then crawls through grass, or other vegetation, gradually peeling back the skin. It is usually shed in one piece, and is inside-out by the time it comes away.

and then once a month. As the snake grows older its rate of growth slows, and then the skin is shed about four times a year.

A Long Life?
It is thought that only a small number of snakes that are born survive the first year.

In order to tell how long snakes can live in the wild, scientists have to mark individual snakes and then record every time a snake is spotted. But this sort of experiment does not always produce accurate results. Many of the snakes are never spotted again after they have been marked, and so the scientists cannot tell what has happened to them.

Another way of learning how long snakes live is by keeping them in captivity. But these results do not take into account that snakes are hunted, or can die of disease or starvation in the wild.

WHERE SNAKES LIVE

Snakes live in many parts of the world. As far north as Canada and as far south as Australia, and most countries in between. Snakes differ in shape, size, colour and behaviour depending on where they live.

Temperature Control

Although snakes, like humans, are vertebrates, they are also reptiles. All of which are often called 'cold-blooded'. This does not mean that a snake's blood is always cold - at times their blood is almost the same temperature as our own. The reason for this name is that reptiles cannot generate heat from within their own bodies. We use up a great deal of energy keeping our bodies at a constant temperature whatever the weather. Snakes, however, can only change their temperature by moving from hot to cold places, or from cold to hot.

Each species of snake has its own preferred body temperature. This is the temperature that the snake's bodily functions are best carried out. If the temperature is too cold, the chemical reactions that drive

▶ The sand viper is from Southern Europe and needs to shelter from the heat at midday in the summer.

▶ The ground boa comes from a tropical region and has no problem keeping itself warm at all times.

a snake's body will slow down – and in extreme cases stop altogether, in which case the snake will die. If the temperature is too hot, the reactions will run out of control and the snake will die of heat exhaustion.

Snakes In Warm Countries

Most snakes function best in temperatures between 25 and 30°C. If a snake happens to live in a place where this is the normal temperature then the snake has no difficulty keeping warm. This is why tropical countries have so many species of snakes. These include the five biggest and

▲ The adder, from Northern Europe, may spend up to six months in hibernation each year.

the five smallest species of snake, snakes that live in places from deserts to the sea, and from the tops of trees down to underground caves and burrows.

Snakes In Cold Countries

Snakes that live in cooler places have to use a few 'tricks' in order to survive. The most obvious trick is to sunbathe. By lying in the sun snakes can absorb the warmth from the sun's rays,

and many flatten their bodies so that the maximum amount of their body surface is exposed to the sun.

During cool days, snakes in cold places will usually spend most of the time underground. Although most snakes cannot look for food while underground, they are hidden, and are far less likely to be attacked by a predator. During the cold winter months these snakes become totally inactive. Just like bears, they hibernate. By doing this they can survive in a state of very deep sleep, until the warm spring and summer months come around.

By using these tricks, snakes have learned how to survive in very cold places. Some can even live on the highest mountain ranges such as the Alps and the Himalayas.

▲ Many desert snakes are small, and burrow down into the sand to escape from extreme heat.

Surviving In Deserts

Snakes that live in hot deserts use different survival tricks. They must have ways of escaping the hot sun to avoid heat exhaustion, as well as surviving the bitter cold when the sun goes down. But perhaps their biggest problem is lasting for long periods of time without water.

Desert snakes are generally small. This means that they heat up quickly in the morning sun after a cold night. Many species are not active during the hottest parts of the year, they prefer to spend their time underground where the temperature is cooler. In addition, desert snakes are partially nocturnal - they come out onto the surface after the sun has set, but before the sand and rocks have lost all their warmth. By pressing their bodies against the surface of the sand or a rock they can keep their bodies warm.

Living Without Water

Saving water is very important for desert snakes. Their skins are more watertight than snakes that live in damp places. Desert snakes get most of their water from their food, but as they don't have to use energy to keep their bodies warm, they do not have to eat very often.

Most desert snakes live on other reptiles and occasionally small rodents and birds. A favourite trick is to shuffle down into the sand with only their eyes showing, and wait for a small, unwary animal to wander by. Most of the species that use this method have their eyes towards the tops of their heads. Many also have small horns sticking up over their eyes to disguise their outline.

Snakes In Water

Most snakes can swim, and many take to water if they are being chased by a predator. Some snakes spend all their lives in water. These snakes cannot lie in the sun, so they live in tropical places where the water is always warm.

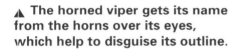

▼ The Asian tentacled snake is found in ditches and rice fields, and rarely ventures onto the land.

▲ The horned viper gets its name from the horns over its eyes, which help to disguise its outline.

These snakes have nostrils near the tops of their heads with valves that close when the snake dives underwater.

Most snakes that live in water give birth to live young, but some come ashore to lay eggs. Sea snakes lay their eggs on seaweed, so that the young do not have far to travel to get back to the sea.

FACT FILE

A snake can survive for about one month on the same amount of food that a bird of the same size needs every day!

WHERE SNAKES LIVE

Underground Snakes

Many species of snakes live a burrowing existence. These range from species that burrow occasionally to others that live entirely underground. Like snakes that live underwater, burrowing snakes cannot bask in the sun to warm up. Instead they move through layers of soil searching for an area that has been warmed by the sun if they are cold, or a patch that is in the shade if they are too hot. Generally speaking burrowing snakes are found in warm parts of the world where there is no need to come to the surface to bask. They are therefore found in deserts, warm grasslands and tropical rainforests.

Burrowing snakes are often short and stout, with a blunt tail. Their heads are usually powerfully built so that they can force their way through the sand and soil. The scale covering the tip of their snouts may be shaped into a 'tool' for burrowing. Burrowing snakes either make their own burrows as they move about underground, or they may take over burrows made by other animals. However, snakes that live in sand dunes sometimes have no burrows at all. These snakes move quickly through the loose sand as if they were swimming.

The more highly specialized burrowing snakes, such as thread snakes, spend most of their lives in termite nests or deep down in forest vegetation. Because they do most of their hunting by smell, these kinds of snake have very simple eyes through which they can hardly see at all.

Snakes In Trees

Snakes that spend most of their time climbing are usually very long and thin. They need the extra length so that they can reach from one branch to the next. They are thin and therefore light, so that the branches can support their weight.

Again, because the trees stop direct sunlight getting through their branches and

▼ Burrowing snakes, such as this thread snake, usually have shiny scales, small eyes and a blunt snout.

◄ **Flying snakes may use their ability to glide in order to leap from one bush or tree to another.**

FLYING SNAKES

A few species of snake that live in trees have an extraordinary way of moving about the forest. Although they don't literally fly from tree to tree, they can jump great distances. They do this by slowing the rate at which they fall through the air. When in the air, the flying snakes flatten their bodies into a thin curve, and at the same time form a rapid series of "S" shapes. This has the effect of slowing the fall so that the snakes begin to glide. Because these snakes have good eyesight and can accurately judge distances they have no difficulty knowing where they are going to land.

leaves, tree snakes cannot bask to stay warm, nor can they hibernate in trees if it gets cold. This is why most species can only survive in tropical places where the air is warm enough for the snakes to function properly.

Most snakes that live in trees hunt small birds, lizards, frogs and even bats. Because these types of animal can move quickly, tree snakes have good eyesight to make sure they catch their prey first time. Many species have special eyes that are excellent at judging distances. In addition, these snakes have slightly longer teeth than most other types of snake. Often the teeth are curved backwards to get a better grip on the prey.

SNAKES AND PEOPLE

◄ **Snake charmers are a popular attraction in parts of Africa and the Miidle East.**

otherwise poor diet. They also worshipped mythical snakes which they believed were responsible for the creation of the world and seasonal rains.

The Greek and Roman god of medicine and healing, Aesculapius, used the snake as a symbol of health and re-birth. Today this design is used in many countries as the emblem of the medical world.

Man's fascination with snakes may have started from the mysteries of their habits. After all, snakes are capable of moving quickly on and under the ground, through trees and water - all without legs. Their gliding movements are beautiful but mysterious. Because of their long narrow shape, snakes will appear where they have never been seen before, and disappear from apparently escape-proof cages.

The way in which a snake sheds its skin is also of great interest. One moment the snake is dull, and the next it is highly colourful. Many tribes see this as a form of re-birth, a secret that people all over the world have been searching for.

Myths And Legends
Western civilizations tend to dislike snakes, but there are cultures that worship them. In the West Indies snakes play a large part in voodoo. This started in Africa, and was taken to the West Indies along with the slaves. The Australian Aborigines ate snakes because of their

The connection between snakes and rain was also part of the snake worship performed by the Hopi Indians of North America. They put snakes into the cracks of rocks, hoping that the snakes would take messages to the rain gods that lived in the mountains.

Ancient Civilizations

Snakes were also a very important part of the religions of other ancient races such a the Egyptians, who worshipped cobras. A rearing cobra's head was a symbol of power. The Greeks and Romans 'borrowed' snake worship from the Egyptians,

▲ Snakes have played a large part in the myths and folklore of people from many parts of the world.

◄ Stylized snakes were often incorporated into the designs used by ancient civilizations.

and used them in their own myths and legends. Medusa, for example, was a hideous monster who could turn people to stone just by looking at them. Her hair was made up of hundreds of live, writhing snakes!

Finally, of course, snakes also play an important part in the Christian religion. It was the snake that tempted Adam and Eve to have a bite of an apple, the forbidden fruit, in the Garden of Eden, and this in turn is what caused God to banish them out of the Garden for ever.

37

SNAKES AND PEOPLE

Well organized mass killings of snakes take place in several states of North America. During these 'rattlesnake round-ups', local people hunt down as many snakes as they can find, often using cruel methods to get the snakes to leave their burrows or dens, killing other animals in the process. The live rattlesnakes are then collected together, teased and tormented, and finally killed. The round-ups date back to the pioneering days, when European settlers wanted to clear land for farms. The snakes were a threat to the people and animals. But this threat no longer exists, and

Man Against Snake

Snakes are widely killed and persecuted by humans. This can be due to a genuine fear that snakes harm people, but more often it is the result of unthinking fear or prejudice. Although only a small number of snakes are dangerously poisonous, many societies look upon all of them with equal hatred. Snakes are killed by agricultural workers who find them in their fields, and by drivers who run them over on purpose when they see them on the roads.

▲ Rattlesnakes are heavily persecuted, even though they are rarely responsible for human deaths.

▼ Irrigation and agriculture are pushing out the highly specialized species which live in deserts.

SNAKE-SKIN PRODUCTS

Snake-skin products like handbags and shoes, are expensive so the skins are worth a great deal of money. This encourages the people of certain countries to hunt them.

Millions of skins are collected every year and exported to wealthy countries. Some species are now legally protected, but it is too late for the ones already extinct.

lakes, developing land for farming and industry, or for people to live on, complete species are being killed off. Sometimes, species become extinct before science has a chance to make a record of them. This tragedy has been taking place for most of this century and there is little evidence of it stopping.

Snakes are often worse affected than other animals because they cannot escape the destruction going on, and become trapped in shrinking areas where they can live. Any remaining snakes that come into contact with the new human population are then killed anyway.

▼ Snakes such as the Madagascan ground boa are endangered and have international protection.

the reason for modern round-ups is just an excuse for a cruel sport.

Habitat Destruction
Killing individual snakes out of prejudice or fear, taking them for their skins, for food or for pets, drastically reduces the number of snakes. But the greatest danger snakes face is the destruction of their habitats. By destroying forests, polluting rivers and

Snakes Against Man

The reason most people give for killing snakes is that they are dangerous to man and a threat to animals. But just how dangerous are snakes?

Out of the 2,500 species of snakes only about 400 belong to the two groups of venomous species, the cobras and the vipers. Of these, less than a half can be considered a danger to people. The rest are either too small, or their venom is not strong enough to cause any great harm. In addition, the most dangerous species are very secretive or rare, and avoid humans.

There are many parts of the world where there aren't any venomous snakes at all. Chile, Madagascar, Ireland, the Canary Islands, New Zealand and most of the West Indian islands are all free from poisonous snakes. Europe has several species of vipers, but few of these are a hazard to human life. In this part of the world, there are on average about 15 people who die through snake bites a year. In the United States, the number is about the same. Even in Australia, where there are more venomous snakes than harmless, only about 10 people die each year.

Accidents in these countries are often the result of bad handling of snakes which would have otherwise been harmless if left in peace. The number of yearly snake bite casualties is very small.

The worst countries for snake bite deaths are those that have dense populations and where many people work on the land.

▲ Many of the 'notorious' snakes, such as the green mamba, only bite humans if they feel in danger.

FACT FILE

● Out of 2,500 species of snakes only about 400 belong to the two venomous groups.
● The most dangerous species are very secretive and avoid humans.

Conservation

Over the last 20 to 30 years, people have become more aware of the damage they are doing to the world. Because of their general unpopularity, snakes have been one of the last species of animal to receive forms of protection. But now countries such as Australia, India, Brazil, Ecuador and many others

◄ The Aruba Island rattlesnake is almost extinct in its natural home, but is bred in fair numbers by zoos.

▲ The Burmese python is a popular 'pet' snake, and used to be collected in large numbers.

have banned the collection and export of their wildlife, including snakes.

In many western countries, some species of snakes have been given total protection. This means that it is illegal to kill them. In Britain, for example, the smooth snake and the adder are totally protected, while the grass snake is partially protected.

In other parts of Europe the laws are even stricter. In Switzerland and Austria all reptiles, such as snakes and lizards, are given total protection.

Although there are efforts being made to protect rare types of snake, there are still many species throughout the world that are in danger of becoming extinct. A recent

survey listed nearly 200 species and subspecies that need some form of protection from man.

In some cases where a species' habitat has been destroyed, or because making laws to protect them is impossible, it is sometimes necessary to save them from extinction by breeding them in captivity, usually in zoos.

41

STUDYING SNAKES

Learning about snakes in the wild is very difficult. Finding them is not easy, even in places where snakes are common. Scientists have to wait hours before interesting discoveries are made.

In cooler countries, snakes are often found basking on banks or logs which face towards the sun. Warm days that aren't too bright are the best days for finding snakes. Species such as the North American garter snake, water snakes and the European grass snake can usually be found near water. These can

▲ Garter snakes are harmless, and may be studied easily by young naturalists in North America.

sometimes be seen swimming on the surface or basking around the edges of lakes. More secretive snakes can

◀ Over most parts of Europe the grass snake is probably the most easily studied species of snake.

studying harmless snakes try weighing them. Many can be recognized by their markings, which can be drawn or photographed. Take temperature readings of the air and ground whenever a snake is seen basking. Notes should be kept of every snake seen, listing its species, size, the exact time and place it was seen, and the weather conditions. Over several years, these records can provide useful information for other, more detailed studies.

sometimes be found by turning over rocks or logs, but care should be taken to replace anything that is moved because other animals may be living there. In places where venomous snakes live, never put your hands beneath these sorts of objects. When in doubt about a snake never try to pick it up.

Records can produce useful information, such as when snakes come out of hibernation, or which species of snakes are found in a particular area, and at what times of the year.

It may be fun to organize a school group. With extra people more complex projects can be attempted. If you are

▼ A perfect place to start studying and learning about snakes is in a zoo's reptile house.

STUDYING SNAKES

Studying Snakes In Zoos

Many zoos in Europe and North America have good collections of snakes. The best ones will also have displays showing items such as snakes' eggs, shed skins and skeletons. Watch how some snakes are out in the open during the day, while others hide. If possible, go back to the cages at different times to see if the snakes have changed position. In this way you may be able to see how snakes control their body temperatures. Watch how they flick their tongues out to 'taste' their surroundings. Do they do this all the time, or only when other snakes go near them?

Look closely at their colouring and markings. Are they camouflaged or do they have warning colours? Try to get as much information from each cage and then try to work out why a certain kind of snake behaves in a certain way. If there is anything you don't understand, ask one of the keepers to explain it.

Keeping Snakes At Home

In recent years, keeping snakes has become a popular hobby. A number of species are available, but not all are suitable for the home. Never attempt to keep a venomous snake. The best species include the cornsnakes, kingsnakes and milksnakes.

Always buy snakes that have been bred in captivity. This stops snakes from being taken from the wild, and also means that it will not have any diseases.

One of the most important things you will need is an escape-proof cage. The best cages are the ones that are

▲ A pet snake can give enjoyment, and stimulate further interest in reptiles and other animals.

▶ The American cornsnake is amongst the most popular pet species; it is attractive and gentle.

designed for snakes. One good type is made out of a wooden box with a sliding glass front. Sometimes a fish tank can be used. Make a wooden lid with wire mesh so that the snake can breathe.

Keeping snakes at the right temperature is essential. A light bulb is no good because

▶ Many pet snakes need a steady supply of mice. If these are not available choose another pet.

▼ A snake cage should be escape-proof and warm. Always include fresh water and a hiding place.

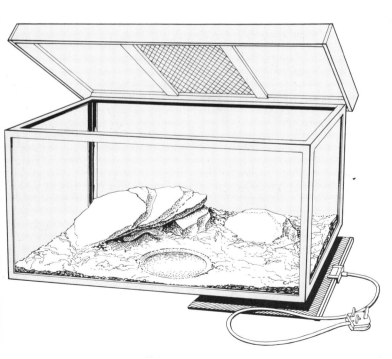

if it is switched off at night then the snake may get cold, but it is equally bad to keep the light on all night. It is best to buy a special heater that fits under one end.

It is not possible to feed a snake with food that it is not used to. Many of the snakes that can be kept feed on mice. If you are not prepared to feed your pet properly and give it the attention it needs, then snake-keeping is not for you. If, however, you can do all the necessary things to keep your snake healthy and happy, keeping snakes is a very rewarding hobby.

INDEX

PHOTOGRAPH CREDITS

The majority of the photographs in this book have been supplied by Chris Mattison.
Other photographs are credited as follows:

Ancient Art & Architecture Collection – page 37 (bottom).
Mary Evans Picture Library – page 37 (top).
Frank Lane Picture Agency – pages 17 (bottom), 36.
Planet Earth Pictures – page 9 (bottom).

Natural Science Photos – front cover (left and top right), back cover; C. Banks pages 33 (top), 41, 44; G. Kinns page 31; Jim Merli title page, pages 11 (top), 12/13, 19, 23, 25 (right), 29; Dick Scott page 8 (top).

PRINTED IN BELGIUM BY
proost
INTERNATIONAL BOOK PRODUCTION